The American Cookbook

The Best Costa Rican Style Recipes to Spice up your Diet

By

Angel Burns

License Notices

Table of Contents

Costa Rican Style Recipes 6

Chapter I - Costa Rican Breakfasts 7

Recipe 1: Costa Rica Breakfast Burrito 8

Recipe 2: Huevos Rancheros – Rancher's Eggs 10

Recipe 3: Panqueques de Banana - Banana Pancakes... 12

Recipe 4: Chipotle Eggs Benedict................................. 14

Recipe 5: Gallo Pinto – Rice & Bean Breakfast 17

Chapter II - Costa Rican Lunch, Dinner Mains and Side Dishes.. 20

Recipe 6: Potato & Egg Enchilada................................. 21

Recipe 7: Spanish Rice.. 24

Recipe 8: Bean & Cheese Empanadas 26

Recipe 9: Sautéed Green Beans with Ham & Garlic 30

Recipe 10: Arroz con Mariscos..................................... 32

Recipe 11: Costa Rican Pepper Steak 35

Recipe 12: Olla de Carne – Beef Stew 37

Recipe 13: Peach-Palm Soup 40

Recipe 14: Sweet Cinnamon Plantains.......................... 43

Recipe 15: Fried Cassava 45

Recipe 16: Marinated Mango 47

Recipe 17: Casado 49

Recipe 18: Ceviche Tico 52

Recipe 19: Black Bean Soup......................... 55

Recipe 20: Stuffed Tortillas 58

Recipe 21: Costa Rica Papas Gallitos 60

Recipe 22: Bacon Chayote Picadillo........................... 62

Recipe 23: Egg Fried Green Beans 65

Recipe 24: Green Rice.................................. 67

Recipe 25: Arroz con Pollo 69

Chapter III - Costa Rica Desserts.. 73

Recipe 26: Pastel de Platano - Banana Cake................ 74

Recipe 27: Tres Leches Cake – Milk Cake................... 76

Recipe 28: Arroz con Leche – Rice Pudding............... 80

Recipe 29: Costa Rican Flan 83

Recipe 30: Cajeta de Coco – Coconut Fudge............... 87

About the Author 89

Author's Afterthoughts.. 91

Costa Rican Style Recipes

HHHHHHHHHHHHHHHHHHHHHHHHHHHHHHHHHHHHHHH

Chapter I – Costa Rican Breakfasts

HHHHHHHHHHHHHHHHHHHHHHHHHHHHHHHHHHHH

Recipe 1: Costa Rica Breakfast Burrito

This breakfast burrito holds the true flavor of Costa Rica. After you try it for the first time, you'll probably find it will be so popular you'll be serving it once or more per week.

Serving Size: 1 Serving

Preparation Time: 10 minutes

Ingredient List:

- 3 & ½ oz. of Gallo pinto (rice and black beans)
- 1 slice of bacon
- 1 egg, scrambled
- 1 tablespoon of cream, sour
- 2 tablespoons of Pico de Gallo
- 1 ounce avocado
- ¾-ounce of cheese, cheddar
- 1 flour tortilla, large

HHHHHHHHHHHHHHHHHHHHHHHHHHHHHHHHHHHHHHHH

Preparation:

1. Put ingredients into tortilla. Order of ingredients doesn't matter. Roll it like a burrito. Seal on plate. Serve.

Recipe 2: Huevos Rancheros — Rancher's Eggs

These are commonly eaten egg dishes in Costa Rica, as well as Mexico. They feature corn tortillas with fried eggs, topped with plenty of beans and cheese. You can add salsa too, if you like.

Serving Size: 2 Servings

Preparation Time: 20 minutes

Ingredient List:

- 1 & ¾ oz. of cheese, cheddar
- 1 & ½ oz. of beans, fried
- 2 tortillas, whole wheat
- 2 eggs, large

HHHHHHHHHHHHHHHHHHHHHHHHHHHHHHHHHHHHHH

Preparation:

1. Fry tortillas and eggs.

2. Spread fried beans onto tortillas and add cheese. Place eggs atop tortillas and spread ranch sauce over all. Serve.

Recipe 3: Panqueques de Banana – Banana Pancakes

This easy recipe may remind you of the tropical weather and exotic flavor of Costa Rica. The miles of plantain and banana plantations are the main reason why they use bananas so well in Costa Rican recipes.

Serving Size: 2 Servings

Preparation Time: 15 minutes

Ingredient List:

- 1/3 fluid ounce of syrup, maple
- 1 cup milk, whole
- 2 cups pancake mix
- 1 fresh banana

HHHHHHHHHHHHHHHHHHHHHHHHHHHHHHHHHHHHH

Preparation:

1. Preheat skillet. Add a bit of oil.

2. Mix ingredients, including bananas, together. Pour into skillet a little at a time, to make individual pancakes. Cook both sides evenly.

3. Serve with syrup and maybe some fresh fruit.

Recipe 4: Chipotle Eggs Benedict

This is an easy recipe, using a lightened chipotle hollandaise sauce. It's ready in less than 45 minutes and makes a great breakfast to give you fuel for the day.

Serving Size: 2 Servings

Preparation Time: 35 minutes

Ingredient List:

For chipotle hollandaise sauce

- 4 tablespoons of butter, melted
- 1 pinch coarse salt
- 2 teaspoons of peppers, chipotle
- 2 teaspoons of lemon juice, fresh
- 2 cgg yolks, largc

For eggs benedict

- 3 slices of ham, cooked
- 4 eggs, large
- 2 English muffins
- To garnish: cilantro

HHHHHHHHHHHHHHHHHHHHHHHHHHHHHHHHHHHHH

Preparation:

For chipotle hollandaise

1. In tall, large glass usable with an immersion blender, add salt, peppers, lemon juice and egg yolks. Cover. Blend for about five seconds. A regular blender will work, too.

2. Pour in butter slowly while blending egg mixture. This will thicken the sauce. After all butter has been melted, add more butter if you like it thicker. Add a bit of warm water if the sauce seems too thick.

3. Keep sauce warm until you're ready to serve.

For eggs benedict

4. Cut the English muffins into halves. Use toaster to brown them. Begin to poach eggs. Once you poach them, place on paper towel. Set them aside.

5. Heat ham in small fry pan on medium-high.

6. Assemble eggs benedict by layering ham slices on top of toasted muffin halves. Follow with poached eggs and dollops of hollandaise sauce. Top with cilantro. Serve.

Recipe 5: Gallo Pinto — Rice & Bean Breakfast

Gallo Pinto is Costa Rica's national dish for breakfast. Its aromatic veggies, rice and beans are topped using eggs. It is most often served as breakfast, but sometimes served at lunch time, too.

Serving Size: 4-6 Servings

Preparation Time: 3 hour & 10 minutes including 3 hours of simmering time for beans

Ingredient List:

- 1-3 tablespoons of oil for frying
- ½ teaspoons of salt, coarse
- 2 cups of rice, white
- 3 cups of broth, chicken
- ½ sweet pepper, small
- 1 pound of black beans, fresh or dried
- 1 onion, small
- 8-10 sprigs of cilantro

HHHHHHHHHHHHHHHHHHHHHHHHHHHHHHHHHHHH

Preparation:

1. Rinse the beans off. Drain. Add one inch of fresh water above beans in pot and bring to boil. Cover pan. Reduce heat to low simmer until the beans are soft. This may take up to three hours. Add some salt.

2. Chop the sweet pepper, cilantro and onion finely.

3. Add the oil to large pan. Sauté rice for two minutes on med-high. Add ½ of onion, cilantro and pepper. Sauté for two more minutes.

4. Add broth. Bring to boil. Cover. Lower heat to simmer until the rice becomes tender.

5. Keep water with the beans to add flavor and color.

6. Sprinkle with cilantro. Serve chilled.

Chapter II – Costa Rican Lunch, Dinner Mains and Side Dishes

НННННННННННННННННННННННННННННННННННННН

Recipe 6: Potato & Egg Enchilada

Some people think of enchiladas as stews and corn tortillas. In Costa Rica, it's a crunchy, soft, delicious puff pastry. The result is a wonderful meeting of aroma, flavor and texture.

Serving Size: 4 Servings

Preparation Time: 70 minutes

Ingredient List:

- 1 beaten egg
- 1 tablespoon of soy sauce
- 1 tablespoon of cumin
- 2 eggs, hard-boiled, chopped
- 1/8 teaspoons of achiote
- 2 cooked, diced potatoes
- 1 & ½ of processed, diced spicy chorizos
- 1 tablespoon of garlic paste
- ½ chopped chili pepper, sweet
- ½ chopped onion
- 4 tablespoons of butter, unsalted
- 8 sheets of puff pastry
- Sea salt & black pepper, as desired

HHHHHHHHHHHHHHHHHHHHHHHHHHHHHHHHHHHHHH

Preparation:

1. Preheat the oven to 350F.

2. Melt butter on med-high in skillet. Cook garlic, onion and chili. Add chorizo. Stir.

3. Stir in achiote and potatoes. Cook for 10-15 minutes or so. Add soy sauce, salt, pepper and cumin. Turn heat off. Add eggs. Set mixture aside.

4. Roll out puff pastry, stretching it out. Cut the pastry into even squares.

5. Place about 2 tablespoons of filling in each. Glaze edges with the beaten eggs.

6. Press square edges together to close.

7. Place on baking sheet. Bake in oven for 40 minutes. Serve hot.

Recipe 7: Spanish Rice

Spanish rice goes great with burritos. This is an especially delicious recipe for the rice. If you want the taste without all the work, this recipe is a great choice.

Serving Size: 4 Servings

Preparation Time: 35 minutes

Ingredient List:

- 2 tablespoons of sugar, brown
- 2 & ¼ cups water, filtered
- 1 & ½ cup rice
- 1 sauce packet (chipotle works well)

HHHHHHHHHHHHHHHHHHHHHHHHHHHHHHHHHHHHHH

Preparation:

1. Stir water, brown sugar and sauce packet together.

2. Add rice to rice cooker. Add sauce mixture. Bring to boil then reduce to simmer. Cover with lid.

3. Allow the rice to cook for about 20 minutes. Use directions on rice cooker to complete. Fluff and serve.

Recipe 8: Bean & Cheese Empanadas

These half-moon baked pockets have a slightly crispy, soft and airy dough. They are full of mozzarella cheese and tender black beans. You can top them with homemade salsa, too.

Serving Size: 12 Servings

Preparation Time: 40 minutes

Ingredient List:

- 1 cup of beans, fried
- 1 chopped onion
- ¼ pound of sausage, chorizo
- ½ teaspoons of Worcestershire sauce
- 4 ounces + 3 tablespoons of oil, vegetable
- ¼ pound of shredded mozzarella cheese
- ½ pound of flour, dough
- ½ pound of flour, corn
- 1 teaspoon of salt, kosher

HHHHHHHHHHHHHHHHHHHHHHHHHHHHHHHHHHHHHHHH

Preparation:

For dough flour

1. Combine salt, dough flour and corn flour in medium bowl. Gradually stir water in until the mixture is smooth. Dough should be a bit sticky.

2. Mix until the edges are fully smoothed. Cover the dough with dampened kitchen towel.

For filling

3. Heat the fried beans in pan on med-high. Add Worcestershire sauce, onions and salt.

4. In another pan, heat chorizo sausage on med-high. Turn meat until it is cooked through.

For turnovers

5. Roll out dough from ¼" to 1/8" thickness.

6. Cut dough into circular shapes of 4-5" in diameter.

7. Brush the rounds using water.

8. Place 1 teaspoon of fried beans, 1 teaspoon cheese and 2 tsp, chorizo sausage on every round.

9. Fold rounds over. Make a rim with a fork, effectively sealing them.

10. Heat 4 oz. of vegetable oil in sauce pan on med-high.

11. Add the empanadas and turn them while cooking until they are lightly browned. Serve them warm.

Recipe 9: Sautéed Green Beans with Ham & Garlic

This recipe uses blanched green beans as its beginning. Then they are sautéed with garlic and butter. It's easy and simple, and it will keep your green beans from becoming too soggy.

Serving Size: 4 Servings

Preparation Time: 25 minutes

Ingredient List:

- 4 slices of prosciutto cheese
- 2 peeled, sliced cloves of garlic
- 2 oz. of olive oil, Spanish
- 6 oz. of green beans, fresh

HHHHHHHHHHHHHHHHHHHHHHHHHHHHHHHHHHHHHHH

Preparation:

1. Put garlic and olive oil in sauté pan. Heat on med. until garlic starts to lighten into a golden color. Don't cook long enough to burn your garlic.

2. Add green beans without stirring them. Allow to cook until they have just started to become softer. This takes five minutes or so. Season with salt as desired.

3. Remove pan from heat. Toss in shredded cheese. Serve.

Recipe 10: Arroz con Mariscos

This dish is delicious, yet fairly quick and easy to make. Once you've made it once or twice, you can make any adjustments you might like to tweak it for you and your family or guests.

Serving Size: 2-4 Servings

Preparation Time: 1 hour & 10 minutes

Ingredient List:

- ½ teaspoons of turmeric – the main taste ingredient in this dish
- 1 tablespoon of chopped parsley
- ¼ cup green peas, frozen
- ½ cup oil, vegetable
- 2 & ½ cups water, filtered
- 1/3 cup medium chopped carrots
- ½ cup chopped pepper, red
- 1/3 cup chopped tomatoes
- 1 cup of chopped onions
- 4 chopped garlic cloves
- 1 & ½ cups rice, uncooked
- 1 pound of frozen shrimp
- 2 & ¾ teaspoons of salt, kosher
- 1 teaspoon of pepper, black

HHHHHHHHHHHHHHHHHHHHHHHHHHHHHHHHHHHH

Preparation:

1. In large-sized pot, heat oil. Add turmeric. Add garlic and onions and cook 'til tender. Add carrots, chopped tomatoes and red pepper immediately. Sauté for about 10 minutes.

2. Add shrimp, kosher salt & black pepper. Cook for 10-12 minutes more.

3. Add parsley, rice and water. Bring to boil.

4. When liquid level is slightly below rice level, lower heat to simmer.

5. Cover and allow to cook for 20-25 minutes. Be sure it does not burn.

6. Add peas. Cover for several additional minutes.

7. Serve hot.

Recipe 11: Costa Rican Pepper Steak

The star of this dish is the sauce, absolutely. You may be skeptical at first, since it's made with jalapenos and evaporated milk, but try it. You'll be pleasantly surprised.

Serving Size: 4 Servings

Preparation Time: 45 minutes

Ingredient List:

- 4 T-bone steaks, beef
- ½ cup of milk, evaporated
- 2 tablespoons of butter, softened
- 2 cubes of bouillon, chicken
- 2 to 4 chopped peppers, jalapeno
- 2 chopped onions, medium

HHHHHHHHHHHHHHHHHHHHHHHHHHHHHHHHHHHHH

Preparation:

1. Fry steaks in pan with oil to your desired level of doneness.

2. In another frying pan, add the butter, jalapeno and onions. Cook for a couple minutes.

3. Add chicken bouillon cube and evaporated milk to the pan. Bring it to a boil. Stir often.

4. Reduce heat. Simmer for two minutes or so.

5. Place cooked steaks back in pan with sauce. Heat all the way through.

6. Place the steaks on plates. Pour the sauce over them.

7. Serve with broccoli and rice, if you like.

Recipe 12: Olla de Carne — Beef Stew

This stew is a bit of a take-off from a similar Spanish dish known as olla podrida. This was once the traditional lunch for most people in Costa Rica, and many people still eat it more than one day each week.

Serving Size: 12 Servings

Preparation Time: 1 hour & 5 minutes

Ingredient List:

- 3 peeled, sliced plantains, green
- 1 pound cubed sweet potatoes
- 1 pound of peeled, cubed taro roots
- 5 cubed cobs of corn
- 1 pound of chopped carrots
- 1 pound of peeled, cubed cassava
- 1 cup of cubed potatoes
- 1 pound of cubed beef short ribs
- 1 pound of cubed lean beef
- 8 cups of water, filtered
- Sea salt, as desired

HHHHHHHHHHHHHHHHHHHHHHHHHHHHHHHHHHHHHHH

Preparation:

1. Heat water in sauce pan on med-high.

2. Add short ribs, lean beef & salt. Cook for 15-20 minutes.

3. Add the cassava, green plantains, cobs and carrots.

4. Wait five minutes and then add sweet potatoes, taro roots and potatoes.

5. Cover. Cook for 20-30 minutes on med-high until meat, roots and veggies have cooked to your preference. Serve hot, with rice, if you like.

Recipe 13: Peach-Palm Soup

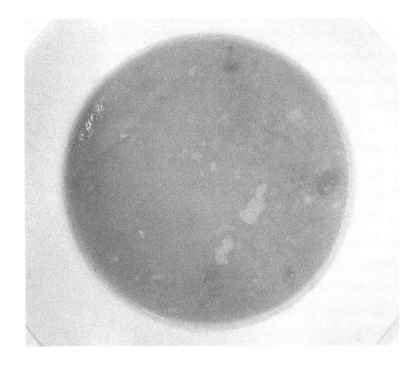

This fruit is common in Central and South America. There are many ways to experiment with the peach-palm fruit, including this soup, as well as salads, stews, tacos and cake.

Serving Size: 6-8 Servings

Preparation Time: 55 minutes

Ingredient List:

- 2 chopped onions, yellow
- 4 tablespoons of flour, all-purpose
- ¼ cup of butter, unsalted
- 1 cup of cream, heavy
- 6 cups of broth, chicken
- 18 peeled, cooked, pitted, chopped peach palms
- 1 sprig each of rosemary and thyme
- 3 bay leaves
- Sea salt & black pepper, ground, as desired

HHHHHHHHHHHHHHHHHHHHHHHHHHHHHHHHHHHHHH

Preparation:

1. In medium pot, melt butter. Sauté onions 'til they start caramelizing.

2. Mix in flour slowly. Add chicken broth and bring mixture to boil.

3. Add the chopped peach palms. Turn heat down. Simmer with bay leaves, rosemary and thyme for about 10 minutes. Then remove the bay leaves and herb bundle.

4. Blend mixture until it is smooth.

5. Simmer 10 minutes longer, allowing it to thicken more. Add sea salt & ground pepper as desired.

6. Garnish using cilantro. Serve hot.

Recipe 14: Sweet Cinnamon Plantains

These fried, sweet plantains are made by pan-frying the banana-like plantain slices until they are tender and warm inside and caramelized and a bit crispy outside.

Serving Size: 4-6 Servings

Preparation Time: 25 minutes

Ingredient List:

- 1 teaspoon of vanilla extract, pure
- 4 to 6 x 1-inch sliced plantains, ripe
- 2 cups water, filtered
- 1 lime, fresh
- ¼ teaspoons of cloves, ground
- ½ teaspoons of nutmeg, ground
- 1 teaspoon of cinnamon, ground
- 1 & ½ cup sugar, granulated
- ½ cup butter, softened

HHHHHHHHHHHHHHHHHHHHHHHHHHHHHHHHHHHHHHHH

Preparation:

1. Melt butter in large-sized pan. Sauté plantains over med. heat, just until they turn golden. Add 1 cup sugar plus vanilla, lime juice, clove, nutmeg and cinnamon. Stir for a couple minutes.

2. Add water. Sprinkle with the rest of the sugar.

3. Reduce the heat to low. Cook until ingredients caramelize. Serve while hot or allow to cool and serve.

Recipe 15: Fried Cassava

This may be your new favorite Saturday treat. If someone in your home won't make it for you, just make it yourself. It's easy to make and the taste is better to some than French fries.

Serving Size: 2 Servings

Preparation Time: 35 minutes

Ingredient List:

- 2 to 3 tablespoons of butter, unsalted
- 1 yucca root, small or medium
- Sea salt, as desired

HHHHHHHHHHHHHHHHHHHHHHHHHHHHHHHHHHHHHHHH

Preparation:

1. Skin yucca root with knife or peeler. Cut into two or three chunks and halve those chunks.

2. Boil yucca root until it's barely soft enough that a fork can poke it. Don't allow it to overboil or it will be too soft and unable to be fried.

3. Remove stringy middle part of yucca, if you see it. If you don't see it, that's fine.

4. Cut yucca chunks into smaller pieces, shaped like French fries.

5. Melt butter in fry pan. Add yucca root. Fry on med-low. Turn the yucca occasionally until browned as you prefer.

6. Salt and serve. Use ketchup to dip in.

Recipe 16: Marinated Mango

This is tasty as the first course at a barbeque. It's great for picnics, or whenever you want a refreshing, cool appetizer. It takes less than a half-hour to make, although it does have about a one-hour time for cooling, too.

Serving Size: 10 Servings

Preparation Time: 1 hour & 20 minutes including 1 hour cooling time.

Ingredient List:

- 2 teaspoons of Worcestershire sauce
- 1 teaspoon of salt, kosher
- 2 tablespoons of chopped onions
- ¼ teaspoons of pepper, ground
- ½ teaspoons of dark, sweet mustard
- 2 tablespoons of ketchup
- 8 to 10 green mangoes, diced and peeled

HHHHHHHHHHHHHHHHHHHHHHHHHHHHHHHHHHHH

Preparation:

1. Mix all ingredients together. Place in refrigerator 'til chilled.

2. Serve soda crackers first, if desired.

3. Garnish bowl with parsley or cilantro.

Recipe 17: Casado

This is a classic meal from Costa Rica that will leave you so satisfied. It has home-cooked, delicious flavor. The hearty portions lead some to call it a comfort food.

Serving Size: 4 Servings

Preparation Time: 1 hour & 5 minutes

Ingredient List:

- 1 cup of sliced queso fresco
- 4 hard-boiled eggs
- 3 cups of cooked beans, black
- 4 pork chops
- 3 cups of cooked rice, white
- 1 grated carrot
- 1 tomato, sliced
- 1 head iceberg lettuce, small
- 2 peeled, sliced plantains, ripe
- ½ cup of broth, beef
- Vegetable oil
- 2 crushed cloves of garlic
- Tortillas to serve
- Vinaigrette for salad dressing
- Sea salt & ground pepper, as desired

HHHHHHHHHHHHHHHHHHHHHHHHHHHHHHHHHHHHHHH

Preparation:

1. Season pork chops with garlic, salt and ground pepper.

2. Heat 2 tablespoons of veg. oil in large-sized skillet on med. heat. Cook chops as you desire on both sides.

3. Deglaze same pan by creating sauce from drippings. To do this, you will add ½ cup of beef broth and bring the drippings to boil. Allow them to reduce to about 1/3 of a cup, then set them aside.

4. Use another fry pan to fry sliced plantains in oil until they are golden brown in color.

5. Combine tomato slices and grated carrot. Use sea salt, ground pepper and vinaigrette to season. Set salad aside.

6. Place chops and extras on four plates. Have tortillas ready, too. Serve promptly.

Recipe 18: Ceviche Tico

I couldn't have a collection of Costa Rican recipes without including a ceviche dish. It's a magical treat that so many people in the country adore.

Serving Size: 4 Servings

Preparation Time: 3 & ½ hours

Ingredient List:

- 2 fluid ounces of ginger ale
- 1 chopped red pepper, sweet
- ½ diced red tomato
- 8 limes, juice only
- ¼ cup of diced or chopped pepper, hot
- ½ chopped onion, red
- 3 minced garlic cloves
- 1 pound of white fish
- 3 tablespoons of raw cilantro, as desired

HHHHHHHHHHHHHHHHHHHHHHHHHHHHHHHHHHHHHHH

Preparation:

1. Chop/mince tomato (no seeds or juice), red pepper, hot pepper, cilantro, garlic and onion. Place in a NON-plastic container. Combine well.

2. Juice limes.

3. Cut fish into pieces of ½ inch each.

4. Mix in fish with other ingredients.

5. Cover with ginger ale and lime juice.

6. Mix well. Be sure fish is completely covered in liquid.

7. Refrigerate for several hours. Mix ceviche every ½ hour to 40 minutes.

8. Add hot sauce, as desired.

9. Serve with plantain chips, tortilla chips or crackers.

Recipe 19: Black Bean Soup

This soup is so simple to make, but it has so much flavor. It tastes even better when you reheat the leftovers the day after it's made. It has a pleasing coriander and cumin taste.

Serving Size: 8 Servings

Preparation Time: 55 minutes

Ingredient List:

- ½ teaspoons of allspice
- ¼ teaspoons of cloves
- ½ teaspoons of cayenne
- ¼ teaspoons of nutmeg
- ¾ teaspoons of powdered coriander
- ½ teaspoons of thyme
- ¾ teaspoons of celery salt
- 1 teaspoon of cumin, ground
- 1 teaspoon of oregano
- 3 cups of stock, vegetable
- 4 x 15-ounce cans of black beans, including their liquid
- 1 tablespoon of oil, olive
- 1 teaspoon of minced ginger, fresh
- 1 teaspoon of minced garlic, fresh
- 1 cup of chopped tomato, fresh
- 1 diced red pepper, medium
- 1 diced medium onion, sweet
- 1 cup of diced celery
- Sea salt, as desired

HHHHHHHHHHHHHHHHHHHHHHHHHHHHHHHHHHHHHH

Preparation:

1. Sauté the ginger, garlic, tomatoes, pepper, onion and celery in oil on med. heat in stock pot until onion is translucent and veggies are tender.

2. Add the rest of the ingredients. Then bring to boil. Simmer for ½ hour and serve hot.

Recipe 20: Stuffed Tortillas

This is such a great recipe to make when you have left leftovers you'd like to use up, like pork, chicken, beef or many kinds of veggies. It's a cheap dish and quite tasty.

Serving Size: 20 Servings

Preparation Time: 20 minutes

Ingredient List:

- Banana peppers, hot, pickled
- 30 tortillas, corn
- 1 pound of beef or poultry
- Sea salt & ground pepper

For cabbage salad

- 2 teaspoons of olive oil, light
- 2 teaspoons of fresh lemon juice
- 3 tablespoons of chopped coriander
- 1 cup of tomato, diced
- 2 cups of shredded cabbage
- Sea salt & ground pepper

HHHHHHHHHHHHHHHHHHHHHHHHHHHHHHHHHHHHH

Preparation:

1. Mix cabbage salad ingredients together. Make immediately before tortillas are served.

2. Place tablespoons of shredded meat on warmed tortilla and top with cabbage salad.

3. Top with hot peppers, as desired.

4. Roll tortillas. Serve.

Recipe 21: Costa Rica Papas Gallitos

People who have visited Costa Rica are happy to take this recipe home with them. Even if you've never been there, you'll love it. It's a typical side dish, with its cooked potatoes on corn tortillas.

Serving Size: 4 Servings

Preparation Time: 40 minutes

Ingredient List:

- 2 teaspoons of coriander, chopped
- 4 tortillas, corn
- 1 teaspoon of paprika
- 1 teaspoon of sugar, granulated
- 3 tablespoons of oil, vegetable
- 2 chopped cloves of garlic
- 3 potatoes, large

HHHHHHHHHHHHHHHHHHHHHHHHHHHHHHHHHHHHHHH

Preparation:

1. Peel the potatoes. Dice into little cubes.

2. Sauté garlic in oil in fry pan. Add 1 teaspoon or so of salt.

3. Add paprika, potatoes and sugar.

4. Cover pan. Cook over med-low for 20 minutes or so. Add water if needed so that the potatoes don't stick.

5. Remove. Serve on corn tortillas (prewarmed, if desired).

Recipe 22: Bacon Chayote Picadillo

This is a dish that many young students in Costa Rica enjoy often. In this country, each version commonly includes the name of the veggie that is the main dish ingredient.

Serving Size: 2-4 Servings

Preparation Time: 55 minutes

Ingredient List:

- 3 tablespoons of butter, unsalted
- 8 strips of bacon
- 2 chayote, whole
- 1 & ½ cups of corn, frozen
- 1 tablespoon of ground cumin
- 2 teaspoons of pepper, ground
- 2 teaspoons of salt, kosher
- 1 tablespoon of Cajon seasoning mix
- 1 Chorizo, Argentinian
- 1 cup of cilantro, fresh
- 2 celery stalks
- 2 bell peppers, medium
- 5 garlic cloves
- 1 medium onion, yellow

HHHHHHHHHHHHHHHHHHHHHHHHHHHHHHHHHHHH

Preparation:

1. Wear gloves to peel the chayote & remove the pit. Slice into ¾" pieces. Place in medium pot. Cover chayote completely. Boil for 15 minutes. Then drain and set the chayote aside.

2. Fry the bacon in frying pan. Turn occasionally. Don't burn it. Remove bacon from the pan and let cool, then break into smaller pieces.

3. Peel & dice onion. Mince garlic. Chop bell pepper into little pieces.

4. In pan with the bacon grease, add the chorizo, celery, bell pepper, garlic and onion. Cook on med-high until a bit soft. Break up chorizo as it is cooking.

5. Add in the cumin, black pepper, Cajun seasoning, chayote, cilantro, butter and corn. Combine well. Add salt as desired. Serve.

Recipe 23: Egg Fried Green Beans

This dish features blanched green beans that are deep-fried to a wonderful crispness that is quite hard to resist. It tastes especially great with ranch dressing.

Serving Size: 2 Servings

Preparation Time: 40 minutes

Ingredient List:

- 2 medium eggs
- 1/3 cup olive oil, light
- 1 tablespoon of flour, all-purpose
- 30 washed green beans with ends trimmed off
- Sea salt, as desired
- 1 teaspoon of cayenne pepper

HHHHHHHHHHHHHHHHHHHHHHHHHHHHHHHHHHHHHHH

Preparation:

1. Boil green beans in salted water in medium sauce pan until they are al dente.

2. Separate eggs – yolks in one bowl and whites in another. Then beat whites until they stiffen slightly. Add yolks, salt & flour. Mix well.

3. Make bunches of six green beans each. Soak them in the batter. Fry in olive oil over med-high heat. Turn after two minutes of cooking.

4. Place in hot oven and cook remainder. Serve promptly.

Recipe 24: Green Rice

This doesn't sound like it would be an especially tasty dish, but if you try it, you may become a fan, too. The taste is much like the rice used in Costa Rican salads and burritos.

Serving Size: 4 Servings

Preparation Time: 40 minutes

Ingredient List:

- 3 cups of broth, chicken
- 1 & ½ cups of long-grain, white rice
- 1 tablespoon of butter, softened
- 1 medium onion
- Sea salt, as desired
- 1 x 2-oz. can of chilies, green
- ½ cup of fresh cilantro
- 2 to 3 minced cloves of garlic
- 2 tablespoons of lime juice

HHHHHHHHHHHHHHHHHHHHHHHHHHHHHHHHHHHHHHH

Preparation:

1. Chop the herbs and vegetables coarsely. Fry in a tablespoon of butter.

2. Add the rice.

3. Stir and coat evenly.

4. Add lime juice, broth and salt. Next, bring to rapid boil and then turn down low. Cover. Simmer for 15-20 minutes or so. DON'T stir. After the 20 minutes, you can fluff the rice with your fork. Serve hot.

Recipe 25: Arroz con Pollo

Chicken and rice is among the most popular of recipes in Costa Rica. It can be served for lunch or dinner. It's easy to find at many restaurants in the country, served alongside salads, French fries or potato chips.

Serving Size: 12 Servings

Preparation Time: 1 hour & 10 minutes

Ingredient List:

For chicken

- 1 celery rib
- 2 garlic cloves
- 2 tablespoons of oil, vegetable
- 1 pound of chicken – half-breasts, wings, thighs or drumsticks
- Sea salt, ground pepper, cumin and oregano as desired

For rice

- 1 x 15-ounce can of drained peas
- 2 sliced carrots
- 2 tablespoons of oil, vegetable
- 1 pound of rinsed, dry, long grain rice, uncooked
- Sea salt, as desired
- 1 teaspoon of annatto (natural food coloring)

For sauce

- 1 x 15-ounce can of tomato paste
- 2 teaspoons of Salsa Lizano (light brown sauce)
- 2 tablespoons of chopped cilantro
- 1 tomato, ripe
- ½ cup of chopped bell pepper, red
- ½ cup of chopped onions

HHHHHHHHHHHHHHHHHHHHHHHHHHHHHHHHHHHH

Preparation:

For chicken

1. Heat oil in sauce pan on med-high. Add chicken (de-boned), along with celery, cumin, oregano, garlic, sea salt & ground pepper.

2. Turn chicken occasionally until it has turned evenly golden brown.

For rice

1. Heat oil in heavy, medium-sized sauce pan on med. heat. Add the rice and stir frequently until the rice has browned slightly.

2. Add salt, carrots and annatto. Add 1 & ¼ qt. of water.

3. Bring the mixture to boil on med-high. Cover. Simmer until rice has become tender. Remove from heat. Leave the rice in the covered sauce pan for about 10 minutes.

For sauce

1. Sauté the Lizano sauce, cilantro, tomato, bell peppers and onions on med. heat in sauce pan.

2. Add the tomato paste. Stir until the sauce is done. Combine the chicken & sauce in sauce pan for two minutes on low heat.

3. Stir in the peas and rice. Cover. Cook for about five minutes. Serve hot.

Chapter III – Costa Rica Desserts

HHHHHHHHHHHHHHHHHHHHHHHHHHHHHHHHHHHHHH

Recipe 26: Pastel de Platano – Banana Cake

This is perfection in dessert form. Many people who eat it will ask you for the recipe. There are many kinds of banana cakes, in countries all over the world, but this is one of the best you'll find, no matter how much you travel.

Serving Size: 24 at 2 inch x 2 inch Servings

Preparation Time: 1 hour & 5 minutes

Ingredient List:

- ¾ cups of sugar, granulated
- 1 teaspoon of vanilla extract, pure
- ½ cup of melted and cooled butter
- 2 & 1/3 cup of ripe bananas, mashed
- 1 teaspoon of nutmeg, ground
- 2 eggs, large
- 1 teaspoon of cloves, ground
- 2 cups of flour, all-purpose
- 1 teaspoon of baking soda

HHHHHHHHHHHHHHHHHHHHHHHHHHHHHHHHHHHHH

Preparation:

1. Sift spices, flour and baking soda together.

2. Mash bananas in separate bowl.

3. Add vanilla, milk, eggs, sugar and butter.

4. Fold dry ingredients into wet mixture.

5. Bake in 13x9" pan for 45-50 minutes. Serve warm.

Recipe 27: Tres Leches Cake – Milk Cake

This is an airy, light sponge cake that gains the texture and taste from three types of milk –heavy cream, evaporated milk and sweetened condensed milk. You'll love the delicious results.

Serving Size: 6-10 Servings

Preparation Time: 3 hours & 45 minutes

Ingredient List:

- 1 tablespoon of rum, dark
- 1 cup of milk, sweetened, condensed
- 1 cup of cream, heavy
- 1 cup of milk, skim, evaporated
- ½ cup of milk, whole
- 2 & ½ teaspoons of vanilla extract, pure
- 3 egg yolks, large
- 1 & ½ cups of sugar, granulated
- 6 egg whites, large
- ¼ teaspoons of cinnamon, ground
- 1 tablespoon of baking powder
- 1 & ½ cups of flour, all-purpose, + extra
- Butter, unsalted

HHHHHHHHHHHHHHHHHHHHHHHHHHHHHHHHHHHHHHH

Preparation:

1. Preheat the oven to 350F.

2. Flour and butter inside walls and inside bottom of cake pan. Set it aside.

3. Whisk 1 & ½ cups of flour, plus cinnamon and baking powder in large bowl.

4. Beat egg whites in separate bowl with an electric mixer until they form firm peaks. Beat in sugar gradually.

5. Add the egg yolks slowly, beating and blending between each addition. Beat in 2 teaspoons of vanilla extract.

6. Add flour mixture in three separate additions. Alternate with milk in two additions, and beginning and ending using flour mixture. Pour the batter into cake pan and smooth the top.

7. Bake the cake for 25 minutes. Reduce oven heat to 325F.

8. Continue to bake until the cake is a golden brown in color. Allow the cake to cool in the pan for about 15 minutes. Invert the cake on a wire rack positioned on a baking sheet.

9. Whisk evaporated milk, ½ teaspoons of vanilla extract and the rest of the ingredients in medium bowl. Use a skewer to poke holes in top of cake.

10. Drizzle half of the sauce over the cake. Allow liquid to soak in each time before you add more. Allow the cake to sit for about 10 minutes.

11. Invert a large plate on the top of cake. Lift rack. Invert cake gently onto the plate. Drizzle the rest of the sauce on the top. Serve.

Recipe 28: Arroz con Leche – Rice Pudding

Some rice pudding recipes have boiled or baked puddings. Others feature a rice pudding that isn't sweet, and which is used for dinner. It's a traditional and popular dish not only in Costa Rica, but also in Panama, Venezuela, Portugal and Spain.

Serving Size: 2-3 Servings

Preparation Time: 40 minutes

Ingredient List:

- 6 cloves
- ½ cup of raisins
- 1 teaspoon of nutmeg, fresh
- 2 cinnamon sticks
- ½ teaspoons of vanilla extract, pure
- ½ cup water, filtered
- 4 cups of milk, whole
- 1 can of milk, evaporated
- 1 can of milk, sweet and condensed
- 1 cup of rice, uncooked

HHHHHHHHHHHHHHHHHHHHHHHHHHHHHHHHHHHHHHH

Preparation:

1. Bring cloves, nutmeg, cinnamon, water, whole milk and rice to boil on high heat.

2. Boil for five minutes. Stir constantly.

3. Add sweetened condensed milk. Simmer on low for 10 minutes.

4. Add raisins, evaporated milk and vanilla extract. Cook for 10 minutes longer, until mixture thickens up. It will thicken more when it cools, too.

5. Serve at room temp or chilled.

Recipe 29: Costa Rican Flan

If you want a traditional Central American treat, you'll want to sample the flan they make in Costa Rica. This dish is delicate and silky, and you can pair it with lots of toppings, from whipped cream to fresh fruit and chocolate chips.

Serving Size: 8 Servings

Preparation Time: 4 hours & 50 minutes including 4 hours of chilling time

Ingredient List:

- ¼ cup + 1 tablespoon of rum, dark
- 8 oz. of chopped chocolate, bittersweet
- 2 tablespoons of corn syrup, dark
- 1 & ¼ cups of cream, whipping
- 2 teaspoons of gelatin, unflavored
- 1 cup of cream, sour
- 1 teaspoon of vanilla extract, pure
- 1 cup of milk, coconut
- 1 tablespoon espresso powder, instant
- ½ cup of brown sugar, dark
- For garnishing: 8 sprigs of mint, fresh

HHHHHHHHHHHHHHHHHHHHHHHHHHHHHHHHHHHHH

Preparation:

1. Sprinkle unflavored gelatin in ¼ cup dark rum. Allow it to soften for about five minutes.

2. Stir 1 & ¼ cups of whipping cream with espresso powder and brown sugar together in sauce pan on med-high.

3. Bring to simmer. Stir until the brown sugar dissolves. Remove from the burner. Whisk in the gelatin mixture until it has dissolved.

4. Whisk in sour cream, coconut milk and vanilla extract until the mixture is smooth. Divide mixture evenly in eight x ¾ cup molds or custard cups.

5. Cover cups with cling wrap. Chill four hours at least or just chill overnight.

6. Bring ¾ cup of whipping cream, along with corn syrup, to simmer on med-high. Once it simmers, remove it from heat. Stir in chocolate until smooth and melted. Stir in 1 tablespoon of rum. Set aside.

7. Run knife around each mold edge. Set each in shallow hot water bowl for about 10 seconds, so they will loosen. Invert mold on serving plate. Remove panna cotta. Spoon some chocolate sauce around each one and use sprigs of mint to garnish.

Recipe 30: Cajeta de Coco – Coconut Fudge

This dessert is simply heavenly. You can't just slice it like you can with chocolate fudge, but it is so delicious, and a great way to indulge yourself – you deserve it.

Serving Size: 20 to 30 balls

Preparation Time: 40 minutes

Ingredient List:

- ½ teaspoons of vanilla, pure
- ½ cup of graham cracker crumbs
- 1 cup of butter, unsalted
- 1 cup of shredded coconut
- 2 cups of milk, sweetened condensed

HHHHHHHHHHHHHHHHHHHHHHHHHHHHHHHHHHHHHHH

Preparation:

1. Combine all ingredients in pan. Cook on low and stir consistently. Cook for five more minutes after it starts boiling.

2. Remove from heat. As soon as mixture is sufficiently cool to handle, use your hands to form small balls and place them in paper cups. Store in a sealed container. Serve when desired.

About the Author

Angel Burns learned to cook when she worked in the local seafood restaurant near her home in Hyannis Port in Massachusetts as a teenager. The head chef took Angel under his wing and taught the young woman the tricks of the trade for cooking seafood. The skills she had learned at a young age helped her get accepted into Boston University's Culinary Program where she also minored in business administration.

Summers off from school meant working at the same restaurant but when Angel's mentor and friend retired as head chef, she took over after graduation and created classic and new dishes that delighted the diners. The restaurant flourished under Angel's culinary creativity and one customer developed more than an appreciation for Angel's food. Several months after taking over the position, the young woman met her future husband at work and they have been inseparable ever since. They still live in Hyannis Port with their two children and a cocker spaniel named Buddy.

Angel Burns turned her passion for cooking and her business acumen into a thriving e-book business. She has authored several successful books on cooking different types of dishes using simple ingredients for novices and experienced chefs alike. She is still head chef in Hyannis Port and says she will probably never leave!

Author's Afterthoughts

With so many books out there to choose from, I want to thank you for choosing this one and taking precious time out of your life to buy and read my work. Readers like you are the reason I take such passion in creating these books.

It is with gratitude and humility that I express how honored I am to become a part of your life and I hope that you take the same pleasure in reading this book as I did in writing it.

Can I ask one small favour? I ask that you write an honest and open review on Amazon of what you thought of the book. This will help other readers make an informed choice on whether to buy this book.

My sincerest thanks,

Angel Burns

If you want to be the first to know about news, new books, events and giveaways, subscribe to my newsletter by clicking the link below

https://angel-burns.gr8.com

or Scan QR-code